Eerie Elementary

The End of ORSON EERIE?

By Jack Chabert

Illustrated by Matt Loveridge,
based on the art of Sam Ricks

BRANCHES™
SCHOLASTIC INC.

READ ALL THE Eerie Elementary ADVENTURES!

1

2

3

4

5

6

7

8

9

10

Table of Contents

To Josh Pruett and family. — JC

Library of Congress Cataloging-in-Publication Data

Names: Chabert, Jack, author. | Loveridge, Matt, illustrator. | Ricks, Sam, artist. | Chabert, Jack. Eerie Elementary ; 10.
Title: The End of Orson Eerie? / by Jack Chabert ; illustrated by Matt Loveridge, based on the art of Sam Ricks.
Description: First edition. | New York, NY : Branches/Scholastic Inc., 2019. | Series: Eerie Elementary ; 10 | Summary: Eerie Elementary is planning a big Halloween-type celebration for Eerie Day, including hosting a "haunted house" at the school itself; but the spirit of the evil scientist Orson Eerie sees this as the chance to finally triumph over the intrepid hall monitors, Sam, Lucy, and Antonio—and it is up to them to prevent a catastrophe and perhaps even defeat Orson and banish him from the school forever.

ISBN: 978-93-90590-19-3

Subjects: LCSH: Haunted schools—Juvenile fiction. | Scientists—Juvenile fiction. | Elementary schools—Juvenile fiction. | Anniversaries—Juvenile fiction. | Horror tales. | CYAC: Haunted places—Fiction. | Scientists—Fiction. | Schools—Fiction. | Anniversaries—Fiction. | Horror stories. | LCGFT: Horror fiction.
Classification: LCC PZ7.C3313 En 2019 | DDC 813.6 [Fic]—dc23 LC record available at https://lccn.loc.gov/2018035384

Book design by Sarah Dvojack
Illustrated by Matt Loveridge
Edited by Katie Carella
First edition, July 2019
This reprint edition: September 2024

Printed in India

ALMOST EERIE DAY

1

"These pumpkins are small!" Sam Graves said. "I wish we were carving huge ones."

Every student in school was gathered in the cafeteria for a special lunchtime activity. They were carving pumpkins for the upcoming Eerie Day celebration. Eerie Day was a local holiday, celebrating the history of the town of Eerie.

Sam's friend Antonio grinned. "Eerie Day is one good thing about living here," he said. "We get, like, two Halloweens each year!"

"And this year, Eerie Day falls on a Friday," their friend Lucy said. "That means we can stay up late! We won't have to rush home! Best of all — it's only two days away!"

"My favorite part is the Eerie Day haunted house!" Antonio said. He leaned over and whispered, "I'm not sure why, but I have a feeling that this year's haunted house will be *extra scary*."

Sam pointed at Lucy's pumpkin and laughed. "Is that one of Antonio's famous sandwiches?"

Lucy nodded. "Yep!"

She had carved the outline of a peanut butter and jelly sandwich into her pumpkin. Antonio always carried a PB and J in his pocket.

"Two can play at that game!" Antonio said. He carved big, round eyes into his pumpkin. "This is how wide your eyes will be at the haunted house — because you'll be so *scared*!"

When Sam looked down at his pumpkin, he gasped. He had unknowingly carved a mustache into it! The mustache curled up like *Orson Eerie's*.

Orson Eerie was the mad scientist who had built Eerie Elementary almost a hundred years ago. He was part of the Eerie family that founded the town. But Orson Eerie didn't deserve to be celebrated on Eerie Day — he was evil! He found a way to live forever — he *became* the school. The school was alive! Eerie Elementary was a living, breathing thing that *fed* on students.

Sam was the school hall monitor. Lucy and Antonio were assistant hall monitors. Together, they kept the students and teachers safe.

Just then, a strange feeling crawled through Sam. As hall monitor, Sam could feel when something bad was going to happen . . .

Suddenly —

Sam's pumpkin leapt off the table! Antonio's and Lucy's did, too!

Students and teachers screamed, "AHHHHH!"

The *pumpkins* were coming to life! Their carved mouths chomped open and closed! Monstrous pumpkins leapt through the air. Some rolled after teachers. Others chased after students.

Antonio exclaimed, "We're under attack!"

PUMPKIN CLASH!

2

The school lunchroom was a battleground! Pumpkins charged after students and teachers!

"What's happening?" Sam yelled, ducking down beside his friends.

"Maybe pumpkins don't like getting carved!" Antonio exclaimed. "I bet they want revenge!"

"The only one who wants revenge," Lucy said, "is Orson Eerie."

Sam, Lucy, and Antonio dashed to the center of the room. All around them, they saw complete chaos!

Students and teachers dove beneath tables! Pumpkins hurled themselves like dodgeballs. They exploded against the walls. Pumpkin seeds filled the air like confetti.

"Monster pumpkins are *everywhere*!" Antonio exclaimed. "How do we stop them?"

Lucy snatched up a lunch tray. She flicked off a glob of mac and cheese, then held the tray high. “We take the pumpkins down,” she said. “One by one!”

“That won’t be easy,” Sam said.

Sam and Antonio grabbed trays. They were ready for battle.

More than a dozen angry pumpkins came bouncing toward the hall monitors.

“They’re closing in!” Lucy shouted.

“From all sides!” Antonio added.

One smirking pumpkin launched itself at Sam. Its orange-fanged mouth chomped.

SNAP! SNAP!

Sam swung the lunch tray and —

The pumpkin exploded. Gooey, stringy bits splattered Sam. An instant later —

PLOP.

PLOMP. PLAMP. FLOMP.

All the pumpkins in the room suddenly dropped to the floor like stones! The battle was over!

Antonio scrunched up his nose. "Um . . . I'm confused. You hit *one* pumpkin, but they *all* stopped attacking?"

Lucy nodded. "That was oddly easy."

"Too easy," Sam said.

Slowly, students and teachers crept from their hiding spots. Some wiped pumpkin seeds from their clothes. Others pulled pumpkin guts from their hair.

Sam's mind raced. *Usually the school attacks in secret. But this time everyone saw! Everyone watched those pumpkins come to life!*

Just then, a voice boomed from the hallway. "Open this door at once!"

VERY SPECIAL EFFECTS

3

Principal Winik burst into the lunchroom. "What happened in here?!" he demanded. He eyed the students and teachers.

Everyone was covered in pumpkin goo.

Before Principal Winik could say anything else, Mr. Nekobi — the old man who took care of Eerie Elementary — rushed over. "Special effects!" Mr. Nekobi called out. "I'm using these pumpkins to test out new Eerie Day effects!"

Sam grinned. *Mr. Nekobi always shows up when we need him!*

Many years ago, Mr. Nekobi had been Eerie Elementary's first hall monitor. He had chosen Sam to be hall monitor. He had told Sam the terrible truth about the school.

"I'll get this cleaned up," Mr. Nekobi told Principal Winik.

The principal flicked a pumpkin seed from his shoe. "Very convincing effects," Principal Winik said. "And they'll have to be . . ."

Principal Winik stepped into the center of the room. "Students, I have news!" he announced. "This Eerie Day, our school will be hosting a haunted hayride on the soccer field!"

Sam looked to his friends nervously. But then —

RING!

"The recess bell!" Lucy said. "Come on!"

Sam started following his friends. He stopped when he felt a hand on his shoulder. It was Principal Winik.

"Sam Graves," the principal said. "The fourth and fifth graders will be building the haunted hayride after school today. Since you are our head hall monitor, would you mind staying late to watch over things?"

Sam nodded. "Sure thing, Principal Winik."

As Sam made his way to recess, he overheard his classmates. Sam was surprised: Everyone believed Mr. Nekobi's special-effects story! No one was talking about the monstrous pumpkins. Instead, they chattered about the haunted hayride — and how exciting it would be to have it *at school.*

But Sam wasn't excited. He was worried. Worried that Orson Eerie was up to something awful . . .

RECESS REASONING

4

Sam, Lucy, and Antonio huddled together on the tetherball court at recess. They were far away from the other students. They needed to talk *serious business*.

"The school has never attacked in such a risky way. And it's never given up so easily," Sam said as he hit the tetherball. "Why now?"

"Orson must be *starving*!" Antonio said. He smacked the ball back.

Lucy dodged the fast swinging ball, then hit it toward Antonio. "If the school is *that* hungry," Lucy said, "a big attack is *definitely* coming."

That sent a chill down Sam's spine. He hit the ball HARD as the bell rang.

Then he followed his friends back to class.

Sam was terrified. Orson Eerie was no longer *hiding* his hunger! That made the monstrous school even more dangerous . . .

The afternoon seemed to drag on forever.

RING! At last, the final bell rang. Sam and his friends stepped outside.

The fourth and fifth graders had begun building the hayride. Some kids moved huge bales of hay. Others set up decorations. Two students drove a small tractor that pulled a wooden wagon.

"Principal Winik asked me to stay until they finish building the hayride," Sam said.

"We'll stay, too," Lucy offered.

"Happy to help!" Antonio added.

Sam laughed. "I can handle this, guys. It'll be a cinch!"

But soon after his friends left, Sam wished they had stayed. He studied the hayride nervously, searching for any sign of Orson Eerie. But all seemed quiet.

By the time the fourth and fifth graders finished the hayride, the sun was setting. Sam waited to make sure no one stayed behind.

Then he set out. He was walking across the soccer field when he heard a loud *creaking.* He looked over at the school. Two jack-o'-lanterns flickered in the windows like eyes.

The school is watching me, Sam thought. *I'm getting out of here — now!*

The shortest route was through the hayride's path. Straw crunched beneath Sam's feet. Bales of hay towered over him. Wind whipped down the path.

Sam jammed his hands into his pockets and walked faster. But soon, he came upon the tractor and wagon. They blocked the path.

That's weird, Sam thought. *The students put the tractor and wagon away . . .* His stomach felt tight. He turned back the way he'd come. *I'd rather take the long way than pass those creepy things.*

KA-KLANK!

Sam looked behind him. The wagon had unhitched itself from the tractor. Its wheels were starting to turn! *A wagon can't move without a tractor — and without someone driving that tractor!* he thought.

The wagon was alive! And it was coming for Sam!

HORRIBLE HAYRIDE!

5

I *need to get out of here!* Sam thought. He quickly ran *past* the tractor. He raced through the hayride, toward the exit.

But the monstrous wagon was hot on his heels. The wagon's rusty wheels sounded like the buzz of an insect. **TSSK! TSSK! KSST!**

Sam saw the end of the path up ahead. *I'm nearly to freedom! Orson Eerie's powers won't work off school grounds!*

But the wheels squeaked louder. **TSSK!** The wagon was catching up! Then —

SLAM!

"Aaaaarrrgh!" Sam cried out. The wagon slammed into him. He tumbled backward into the wagon bed.

Sam gripped the side of the wagon as it took off like a rocket. It whipped around corners. He was nearly flung off as it went up on two wheels. Coming around the next turn, Sam saw the doors to Eerie Elementary swing open.

"No!!" Sam yelled.

The school's doors were like a hungry mouth! Red light glowed inside. Eerie Elementary looked ready to eat — and the wagon was delivering the main course: Sam!

THE END OF THE RIDE

6

The speeding wagon carried Sam toward Eerie Elementary's open mouth.

I'm about to be Orson's dinner! Sam thought.

But then —

GHHHRRAR!

Sam heard an engine growl. He looked around to see where the sound came from. But —

KA-SLAM! Something *hit* the wagon.

"Whoa!" Sam cried. He was thrown from the wagon and landed in a hay pile.

"Hey, Sam!" a familiar voice called out. "Are you starting the Eerie Day celebrations without us?"

Sam blinked. Antonio and Lucy were driving the tractor! They had rammed the wagon!

"Let's take care of that monstrous wagon!" Lucy said as she climbed down from the driver's seat.

But the wagon was no longer monstrous. It lay still. The wheels spun harmlessly. Eerie Elementary's doors slammed shut.

The attack was over.

Sam sagged against a hay bale and caught his breath. "Good timing, guys. But how did you know I was in trouble?" he asked.

"I called to see if you got home okay," Lucy said. "Your mom hadn't seen you, so I called Antonio —"

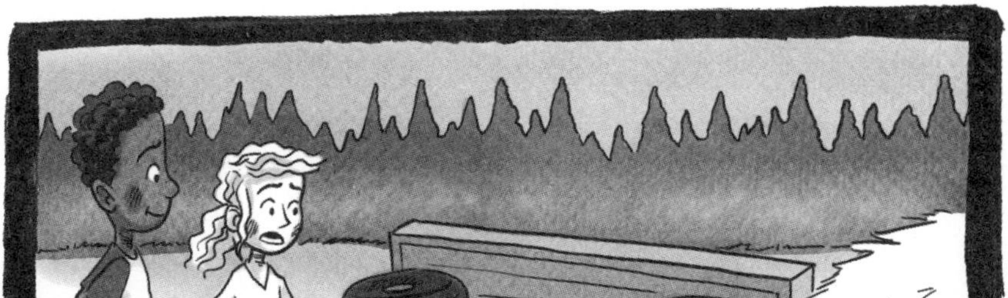

"And I was like, *SAM'S IN TROUBLE*!" Antonio said.

"So here we are," Lucy said with a smile.

Sam shook his head. "That wagon was going to feed me to Orson. But the moment it was hit by the tractor, it stopped. It didn't fight back or anything!"

"That *was* easy," Lucy said as they began walking home. "Just like the pumpkins this morning."

"Two easy battles in a row!" Antonio said. He was almost skipping down the sidewalk. "We're really getting the hang of this hall monitor thing."

Suddenly, Lucy stopped. Her eyes were wide as she grabbed her friends. "Antonio, what happens when you go too long without eating a peanut butter and jelly sandwich?"

"Oh man," Antonio groaned. "I can barely move!"

"Exactly!" Lucy said. "You're *so* hungry that you're *weak*! I think *that's* what's happening to Eerie Elementary. We've defeated it time after time. Now the school is *starving*! We defeated it easily BECAUSE it's weak! And Orson Eerie is getting *desperate*!"

Those words hung in the air . . . It made sense. Sam knew they would have to be braver than ever before . . .

"This is our moment," Sam said. "Now is the time to risk everything. Now is the time to defeat Orson Eerie *for good*."

Lucy and Antonio nodded. But they all had the same thought: *How?*

HAUNTING!

7

It was Thursday morning. Sam, Lucy, and Antonio were sitting in Ms. Grinker's class. The loudspeaker crackled.

It was Principal Winik. "This is a very important announcement about tomorrow's Eerie Day celebration. The haunted house *was* going to be held at Jasper Eerie's mansion, but there has been a change of plans."

Sam glanced at Lucy and Antonio. Jasper Eerie was the great-great-grandson of Orson Eerie. He lived in Orson Eerie's old house. He had been a substitute teacher at Eerie Elementary, and helped the hall monitors more than once . . .

Principal Winik continued, "The haunted house will now be held here . . . inside Eerie Elementary!"

Students erupted with excitement! But the hall monitors knew what this meant. Sam whispered, "No question. Orson Eerie's biggest attack *ever* will be tomorrow night."

"And we'll defeat him," Lucy said. "Once and for all."

"He is so weak — this should be EASY!" Antonio said, grinning.

"All we need now is a plan," Sam added.

The rest of the day was a blur. Lessons were canceled so that students could decorate the haunted school.

When the final bell rang, Sam had an idea. “Let’s go talk to Jasper Eerie,” he said to Antonio and Lucy. “Maybe he’s not hosting the haunted house because he discovered something about Orson Eerie! Maybe he found a weakness we can use!”

“Good thinking,” Lucy said.

The hall monitors headed across town. Eerie Day banners hung from lampposts. Posters were plastered on mailboxes.

Finally, they reached Jasper Eerie's house. It looked creepier than usual. The windows drooped like sad, spooky eyes. The house's splintered wooden body seemed tired.

"Geez. Jasper wouldn't even need to add decorations to make *this* house look haunted," Antonio said.

Sam said, "Well, let's hope Jasper knows something that can help us battle our monstrous school —"

"Which is about to be a haunted house!" Lucy interrupted.

Sam, Lucy, and Antonio walked up the front steps. Sam started to knock on the door when —

Jasper Eerie flung it open and exclaimed, "I saw Orson last night!"

JASPER'S NIGHTMARE

8

"Orson Eerie was here!" Jasper said.

Sam, Antonio, and Lucy nervously looked around as they stepped inside.

"Orson was *off school grounds*?" Sam asked.

"Yes!" Jasper said. "I saw him *in my dreams*. But he was so real! I'm SURE he was here!"

Sam and his friends sighed. It was just a nightmare. Sam wasn't surprised — Jasper was a scaredy-cat. He wouldn't even go *near* the school anymore.

Jasper shakily headed into the kitchen and sat down. Orson Eerie's journals, notes, and diaries were stacked everywhere.

"After I agreed to host the haunted house, I started having nightmares," Jasper explained. "The nightmares got worse as Eerie Day got closer. Last night, I dreamt I was surrounded by Orson Eeries! Like an army!"

Sam gasped. *An army of Orson Eeries!*

Jasper continued. "So I called Principal Winik this morning. I explained I was too frightened to host the haunted house."

We're all *frightened*, Sam thought. *But we can't quit. We have to defeat Orson tomorrow — once and for all!*

"Jasper," Lucy said. "We need your help finding Orson's ultimate weakness. It's the only way we stand a chance."

Jasper shook his head. "I'm afraid I don't have any clue what Orson's weakness is."

"Let's get to work," Sam said. "We must find *something*."

They began reading Orson's old journals and diaries. They searched and searched. Soon, the sun was setting and they hadn't found anything.

Sam sighed. It felt hopeless. But then —

"Look, guys!" Antonio exclaimed. "Orson's journal entry from September 6, 1923! The day the school opened!"

Antonio read the entry aloud: "I will *become* Eerie Elementary. I will live forever by feeding on students. My powers will spread and grow."

Sam shivered.

Antonio turned to the final page. His voice was a whisper as he read the last words Orson ever wrote: "And *nothing* will stand in my way!"

Everyone was quiet.

"But Orson Eerie was *wrong*," Lucy said. "Something *did* stand in his way. Us! The hall monitors!"

Antonio pounded the table. "Right! We've defeated Orson before, and we'll do it again!"

Sam nodded. "But this time . . . we'll need *more*."

"Count me out!" Jasper said. His voice shook. "I'm sorry, but I was scared even *before* I had my nightmare!"

Jasper's terrifying nightmare gave Sam an idea. *An army.*

"I've got a plan!" Sam said. "It's going to sound crazy . . . But if it works, Orson Eerie will be gone forever."

Sam pulled out his hall monitor sash. He gripped it tight and then —

Sam tore his sash in half.

"What are you doing?!" Antonio exclaimed.

Sam was nervous. His plan *was* crazy. He wasn't sure it would work. But he *was* sure Orson Eerie would never see it coming . . .

"Lucy, Antonio: Call your parents. Tell them you'll be home late," Sam replied. "It's going to be a *long* night."

They got to work.

THE FIRST SASH

9

At last, it was Friday: Eerie Day! The morning bell hadn't rung yet — but Sam, Lucy, and Antonio were already in Principal Winik's office. They had to set their plan in motion . . .

"Principal Winik," Sam said. "We'd like to volunteer to lead visitors through our haunted school tonight."

Mr. Winik leaned back. "Hmm. There *will* be lots of people attending: students, teachers, parents, and other townspeople. And as hall monitors, you know this school better than anyone," he said. "Okay, the job is yours!"

The friends exchanged excited glances as they left the office. So far, so good.

Antonio carried a duffel bag. It was full of last night's hard work.

Sam grinned. "Guys, our plan will work if—"

YANK! A hand grabbed Sam! Another tugged Lucy's backpack and the strap of Antonio's bag. They were yanked into the janitor's closet.

This was no ordinary closet. Its rear wall began to move. Soon, a secret door opened and they were in a hidden room. The room was dark. It smelled wet. It was the same room where Sam had begun his journey as hall monitor.

Mr. Nekobi stood in the shadows. "I apologize for scaring you. But secrecy is important. No one can see what I am about to give you."

Mr. Nekobi held a small glass box. It looked like a box for storing a prized baseball. "Tonight, you'll need all the help you can get," he said. "I am too weak for battle. But this might help *you*."

The friends crowded around. "This box contains my hall monitor sash from years ago," Mr. Nekobi said.

Sam leaned in. The orange sash was faded and yet it seemed to glow. It reminded Sam of Mr. Nekobi himself: worn around the edges, but still strong.

"Your sash looks like it's seen some action," Sam said softly.

"For real," Antonio said.

"So cool . . . ," Lucy added.

"Oh yes," Mr. Nekobi said. "But those are stories for another time."

Sam took the box. Holding it, he felt stronger and braver.

"Thank you, Mr. Nekobi," he said. "This might give us the edge we need to defeat Orson Erie once and for all!"

"Let us hope," Mr. Nekobi said. "Now hurry to class. It will be nighttime before you know it."

10
HAUNTED HALLS

The school day was finally over. The three hall monitors stood on the steps of Eerie Elementary. Everyone else was in town enjoying the Eerie Day festivities.

The sun was setting. It cast purple shadows across the school, giving it a spooky glow. The haunted house decorations made the school look creepier than usual.

"Any minute now," Sam said, "Orson will strike."

It had been less than one year since Sam had learned the truth about Orson Eerie — since Sam and Orson became enemies. In that short period, Sam and Orson had battled many times . . .

But if my plan works, Sam thought, *tonight's battle will be our last.*

"Look!" Lucy said, nudging her friends.

Hundreds of people walked across the field. They were drinking lemonade, eating treats, and laughing.

"The parade downtown must be over," said Antonio.

"It looks like everyone is having fun," Sam said. He swallowed. "They have no idea what scary strangeness is about to happen."

Most townspeople lined up for the haunted hayride. But Mr. Nekobi led a group of ten parents and kids to the hall monitors.

Sam glanced over at Antonio and Lucy. He knew they were thinking the same thing: *Everything we've done as hall monitors has led to this moment — to this walk through the school . . .*

Antonio used his best speaking voice to greet the group. "Welcome to the terrifying tour of our haunted school. Welcome to Eerie Elementary!"

Students giggled nervously. Grown-ups smiled.

Lucy opened the front doors. "A mad scientist named Orson Eerie created this school," she said as the group filed in. "Some say he is *still* part of this school . . . and that his evil fills these halls! Prepare to be *scared*! And keep an eye out for monstrous Orson Eerie!"

The hall monitors took turns speaking.

Sam said, "Legend says that *only hall monitors* can stop this monstrous, haunted school."

Antonio held up a shiny sash. Everyone watched. "This orange sash is a symbol of the hall monitors' power."

"Lucy, Antonio, and I are hall monitors," Sam continued. "But tonight, we need an ARMY of hall monitors to help us fight!"

"So tonight," Lucy said, "you will *all* be hall monitors!"

Antonio opened his duffel bag. It was full of brand-new orange sashes. Even with Jasper's help, it had taken the friends all night to sew them.

"These sashes are the only things that will keep you safe," Sam said. "Put yours on before it's too late —"

KLANG!

Suddenly, the doors slammed shut! There was no turning back. The only way out was by defeating Orson Eerie!

11
GREATEST HITS

"Everyone, stick together," Sam told the group. "This is a school of HORRORS! We don't want you to get caught in its evil web."

Sam steered the group down the dark, creepy hallway. Lucy and Antonio followed to make sure there were no stragglers. Kids clung to parents. They all pushed through cottony cobwebs and past paper skeletons.

Sam, Lucy, and Antonio took turns telling scary stories about the school. They spoke of evil pipes, hungry bubble-gum monsters, and living dodgeballs. Only *they* knew the stories were *real.*

"Stay alert!" Lucy told the group. "Orson Eerie could attack at any moment!"

Lucy was right. They entered the gym — and lights flashed.

"Oh my!" someone exclaimed.

A vast volcano was forming inside the gym! The group oohed and aahed. They thought it was all a special effect.

But this volcano was *alive* — just like the one Sam, Lucy, and Antonio had battled at the science fair months earlier.

The hair on the back of Sam's neck stood up. Sam took a deep breath. He and his friends had planned for this . . . But there was no way to *truly* prepare for a battle with Orson Eerie.

The volcano spewed hot lava across the floor. Sam shouted, "Everyone! Show your sashes!"

The group seemed excited and scared. Everyone held out their orange sashes.

The volcano howled! It shrieked! Then —

POOF! It collapsed.

A single puff of smoke drifted from the small crater that remained.

The plan is working! Sam thought. *Orson is too weak to fight an entire hall monitor army!*

Antonio whispered to Sam and Lucy. "These sashes are like cloves of garlic in a vampire movie. Orson can't stand them!"

They continued down the dark hallways. They ducked beneath dangling rubber spiders.

In the art room, a massive clay T. rex snarled and licked its lips! Everyone gasped. It stomped toward the group.

Antonio commanded, "Everyone! SHOW YOUR SASHES!"

The clay creature howled — then melted and disappeared.

The group pressed on.

Orson Eerie appeared again and again — each time in a form they had seen before.

And each time, he was defeated by the power of the hall monitors' army.

"Orson is only taking forms we've seen before," Lucy whispered.

"Because he's weak!" Antonio replied. "He doesn't have enough power to create anything new."

"I can sense him," Sam added. "He is hurting. The sashes frighten him."

Lucy nodded. "We're almost to the end of the haunted house. Then it will be the end of Orson Eerie — once and for all."

But Lucy was wrong. Sam was wrong. They were all wrong. The battle wasn't even close to over . . .

12

NOT SO FAST!

Sam led the group to the final hallway of the haunted house tour. The friends gasped when they saw what waited for them there. An artist's easel stood at the end of the hall. A painting of Orson Eerie stared back at them.

"That painting doesn't belong there," Antonio said.

"It was just hanging in the front hallway!" Lucy added.

"But it's here now," Sam said. "Blocking the way out . . ."

The lights flickered. The hall darkened. Strange shadows ran along the lockers. The group quietly inched toward the exit.

Sam felt the painting pulling him closer, like a magnet.

The painting shimmered, and the colors swirled, as Orson's face came alive. His voice was weak: **"I do not understand . . . How do ALL of these sashes have powers?"**

Sam stepped toward the painting. "I'll tell you how!" he said. "We sewed a piece of *my sash* inside *all of these other sashes*! I've shared my hall monitor powers!"

Orson's painted mouth opened. But his voice no longer came from the painting — it came from *the halls.* **"Do you mean that every one of these sashes contains a piece of YOUR sash?"**

The air turned ice-cold.

Sam heard nervous whispers. He saw that the group was scared — REALLY scared. Orson's terrifying voice had cut through them.

They know something bad is happening, Sam thought. *They know this isn't just part of the tour. They probably want to run.*

Sam understood. Orson's booming voice made Sam want to run, too. But he had a job to do. He *had* to show Orson he wasn't scared.

Sam pointed at the painting. "That's right! You're outnumbered, Orson Eerie!"

Lucy shouted, "You might have many forms —"

"But *we* have many hall monitors!" Antonio added. "Everyone! SHOW YOUR SASHES!"

But not a single sash was waved; the group was scared stiff. The lights flashed faster and faster. Then, suddenly —

CLICK! Everything went dark! The only light was from the moonlight through the windows.

PWFOOM!

A flame appeared. It floated in midair. The flame's heat made everyone take a step back.

"I WILL NEVER LEAVE!" bellowed Orson. **"I AM EERIE ELEMENTARY!"**

The flame grew brighter and hotter. Sam realized what it was becoming . . .

Orson Eerie was taking the form of an enormous pumpkin. But it was a terrifying, jumbled mess of a form. The pumpkin was made from bits of cobweb and creepy decorations. The flame burned within its mouth.

Behind them, a student shrieked.

"It's okay!" Antonio told the group. "This is all part of the haunted house experience!"

Sam doubted anyone believed Antonio. He had seen their fearful faces. Now the monstrous pumpkin charged toward them! He had to get everyone to safety!

"RUN!" yelled Sam.

13
PUMP THE BRAKES!

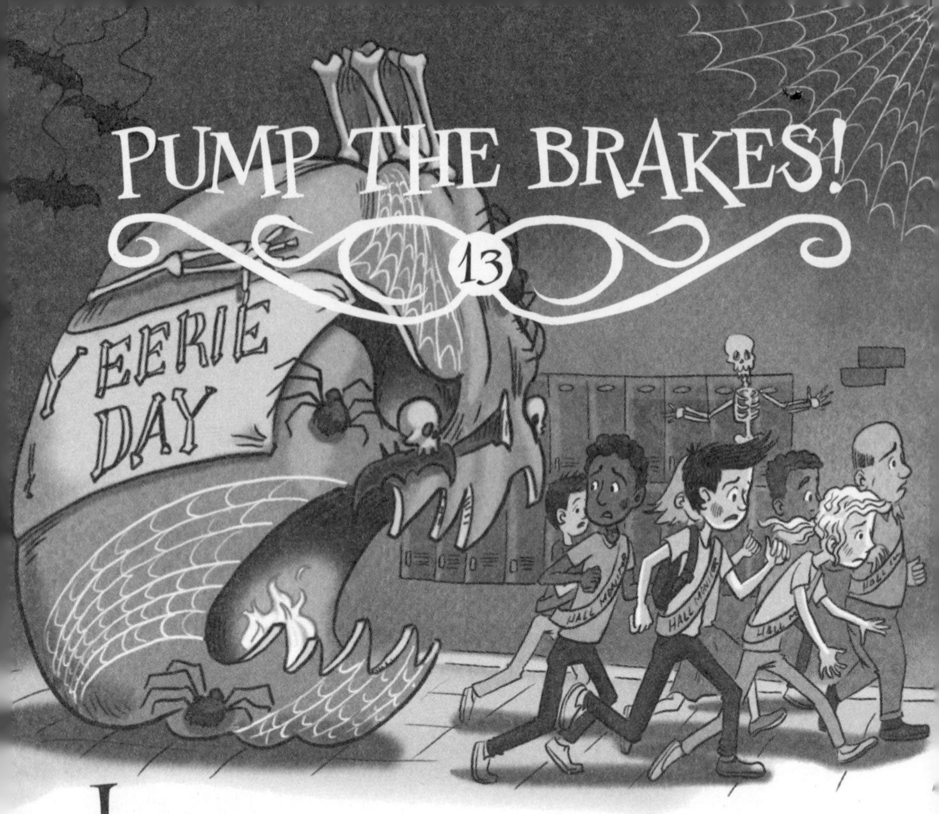

In an instant, the entire tour group was *racing* toward the exit. It was a stampede.

"This way!" Antonio cried, as he flung open the door. The group raced outside to safety. Then —

KLANG!

The door LEAPT from Antonio's hand and snapped shut. He tugged — but it wouldn't budge.

"Come on! We can escape out the main exit," Sam cried, pulling his friends down another hallway.

The pumpkin charged after the hall monitors. Sam raced down the long halls. If they could just stay ahead of the monstrous pumpkin . . . But —

WHAM! BAM!

The huge pumpkin slammed into Lucy and Antonio. They were knocked to the side.

Sam wanted to run back to them. But he couldn't — because the pumpkin was still barreling toward him!

Finally, Sam threw himself into the exit doors. He felt his sash tremble. Orson was growing weaker. Weak enough that —

KLANG! The doors opened!

Sam stumbled down the school steps. He saw people watching. Everyone could see what was happening!

The monstrous pumpkin bounced down the steps after Sam.

Sam scurried backward. "You won't win, Orson."

"Creating more hall monitors was clever, Sam Graves," Orson said. **"But without Lucy and Antonio, you cannot overpower me. You are strong — but not strong enough! Mr. Nekobi was a better hall monitor than you!"**

A thought sprang into Sam's head. *Mr. Nekobi's sash!*

Sam reached into his bag and yanked out the box Mr. Nekobi had given him that morning.

The pumpkin *flinched*. It rolled to a stop.

"What is that?" Orson asked.

Sam opened the box and grabbed the old sash. It felt warm in his hands. There was power in its threads. Sam could *feel* it making him stronger!

The monster's glowing eyes flashed with anger. Then its huge mouth opened wide. Sam felt Orson's hot breath on his face. He closed his eyes and braced for the bite!

SNAGGED!

14

But Orson's bite never came. Sam wasn't pumpkin food! He slowly opened one eye. He was staring into the snapping mouth of the monster! He saw the stringy, dripping insides of the pumpkin.

The Orson pumpkin wrestled and shook. But it wasn't coming any closer. Something held it back!

Sam heard the **RUMBLE RUMBLE** of an engine.

"Assistant hall monitors to the rescue!" Antonio shouted.

"We got him, Sam!" Lucy yelled.

Sam peered around the angry pumpkin. He saw his friends driving the tractor from the hayride. Lucy and Antonio had thrown coils and coils of thick rope around the pumpkin! Some circled around its thick stem. Other coils were tight against the pumpkin's monstrous mouth. Orson was like a dog on a very strong leash!

Sam felt the townspeople watching them.

Orson Eerie must have felt it, too, because he suddenly pulled with *all his might.* He tugged with the strength of elephants!

RAWRRRR! The monster growled.

The tractor wheels spun and the engine smoked! The machine's strength was being tested!

"I WILL NOT BE DEFEATED!" Orson Eerie roared. He pulled harder and harder. The ground cracked. The school shook. Bricks fell and windows broke.

There was one final pull. Lucy and Antonio leapt from the tractor, and then —

SPLURT! The pumpkin tore itself open! Strange, pulpy seeds filled the air! Then a slithery, storm-cloud-like Orson Eerie snaked out of the pumpkin.

The cloud became a thick, gray mist blocking the moon. Then Orson spoke — and his voice came from everywhere. **"I have not even begun to fight!"**

"He's trying to scare us," Sam whispered.

"Well, it's working!" Lucy said, taking a step back.

"But look!" Antonio said, pointing. "The mist is thinning! He's weakening!"

Sam gulped. THIS was their big moment. They needed to finish him off! *Now!*

15
ALL EYES ON ORSON

The Orson Eerie mist swirled.

Sam clutched Mr. Nekobi's old sash. It felt as powerful as a sword.

"We were always the ones who stopped you, Orson!" Sam hollered. "And we always will be — because that's our job. We're hall monitors!"

Memories rushed through Sam's mind. He recalled the many ways he and his friends had used the sash before . . .

The sash was the symbol of their strength and friendship. It was a symbol of GOOD.

"You'll never stop us, Orson! Not with the powers of the sash on our side!" Sam said.

Just then, Mr. Nekobi himself stepped to the front of the crowd. "Everyone! RAISE YOUR SASHES!"

Sam spun around. He saw the townspeople. They looked confused and scared. No one seemed sure what was real and what was not, but they did what Mr. Nekobi said . . .

One parent took a step forward. And then a teacher. And then a student. They all held their sashes high.

A *growl* came from the thick, gray mist. Orson Eerie darted and swirled, but more townspeople stepped forward. More sashes closed in. They formed a semicircle around the mist. Eerie Elementary stood like a wall behind it.

"To beat us, you need a sash of your *own*," Sam said. "Here — I'll even let you have this one. Go on. Just try and take it. *I dare you!*" He dangled Mr. Nekobi's sash in front of the swirling Orson Eerie mist.

Orson's voice boomed: **"Your sash has stopped me before, Sam Graves. But never again! I WILL DESTROY ALL THE SASHES! And I will start with Nekobi's . . ."**

The mist spun closer and closer. Then — WHOOMP!

The sash turned ice-cold as Orson Eerie entered it. It jerked in Sam's hand! The sash whipped about like a kite in a storm.

"I will destroy this sash. Then I will take another form! I will finally FEED! At last my power will spread!"

"I don't think so, Orson," Sam said.

Antonio said, "The sash is a symbol of the hall monitors' responsibility to protect the students!"

"And hall monitors could *never* hurt the school or its students!" Lucy shouted.

Sam smiled. "Now that you are *in* that sash, you can *never* put the students in danger again! You will stay TRAPPED in that sash FOREVER!"

Orson howled in anger! His cries echoed across the field. The sash shook, but it was no use. Orson was imprisoned.

"You tricked me!" Orson yelled. **"This cannot be! I designed this school! I built and painted this school with my bare hands! I <u>am</u> Eerie Elementary! I can't be defeated! I! CANNOT!"**

The hall monitor sash snapped like a whip. Then it fell to the ground.

16

SO LONG, ORSON EERIE

The hall monitors looked down. The sash was limp and lifeless.

Sam bent to pick it up. His fingers grazed the fabric. "Ow!" he cried. "It's hot!"

Lucy opened the glass box. She carefully pushed the sash inside without touching it.

And like that, the battle was over.

Hundreds of faces stared at Sam, Lucy, and Antonio. Parents, teachers, students, and townspeople had all seen them defeat mad scientist Orson Eerie.

Mr. Nekobi approached. He patted Sam on the shoulder, then turned to the crowd. "I hope you enjoyed tonight's haunted house, all the incredibly realistic special effects, and your three amazing guides!"

No one seemed to know what to say. Everyone was stunned.

An unexpected sound broke the silence: applause. Jasper had refused to set foot on school grounds for months, but he was there now! And he was clapping for the hall monitors.

Soon, everyone clapped.

Principal Winik stepped forward. "That was VERY bizarre — but I do believe this haunted house was the best Eerie Day haunted house EVER! Please . . . another round of applause for Mr. Nekobi's special effects and for your guides!"

Mr. Nekobi and the hall monitors stood together. Sam waved awkwardly to his mom.

Finally, the crowd headed home.

Sam saw Principal Winik speaking to Jasper. Jasper was smiling and nodding. Sam guessed Jasper might soon be a full-time teacher at Eerie Elementary.

"I'll take my box," Mr. Nekobi said.

"It's all yours!" Antonio replied, smiling. He handed it over.

"Congratulations, hall monitors. You've done what I could never do. You've defeated Orson Eerie once and for all," Mr. Nekobi said. "Let's head inside and put this box somewhere safe."

The three friends followed Mr. Nekobi inside. The school's walls, the lockers, and the ceiling all seemed brighter. It was as if the school had been sick, but now it was healthy again.

"And that's that," Mr. Nekobi said. He placed the box inside the trophy cabinet.

Mr. Nekobi looked at Sam. Sam sensed there were many things the old man wanted to tell him. But instead, Mr. Nekobi smiled softly and turned.

He walked slowly down the long hall — then disappeared around the corner. Gone.

With Orson Eerie finally defeated, the hall monitors' work was done.

Sam shared a look with Antonio and Lucy. He felt like he should say something — but what? "So, um . . . The past year has been, well . . ."

Lucy scrunched up her forehead. "Scary? Weird? Strange? Fun?"

Antonio laughed. "How about . . . *all of the above*?"

Sam chuckled. "Oh, and one more: an honor!"

Antonio and Lucy both gave Sam a slap on the back. They were happy Orson Eerie was no longer a threat. But Sam had a feeling that, in some way, they would miss being hall monitors.

Sam thought back to the beginning, when Mr. Nekobi chose him. He hadn't wanted to be hall monitor then.

But now?

Now he and Antonio and Lucy had grown so much. Together, they had saved the school and saved one another more times than Sam could count.

What would happen now?

Sam did not know.

The only thing Sam knew was this: If Eerie Elementary ever needed them again, he and Lucy and Antonio would be there.

Friends. Hall monitors. Heroes.

Shhhh!

This news is top secret:

Jack Chabert is a pen name for *New York Times*–bestselling author Max Brallier. (Max uses a made-up name instead of his real name so Orson Eerie won't come after him, too!)

Max was once a hall monitor at Joshua Eaton Elementary School in Reading, MA. But today, Max lives in a super-weird old apartment building in New York City. His days are spent writing, playing video games, and reading comic books. And at night, he walks the halls, always prepared for the moment when his building will come alive.

Max is the author of more than twenty books for children, including the middle-grade series The Last Kids on Earth and Galactic Hot Dogs. Visit the author at MaxBrallier.com.

Matt Loveridge loves illustrating children's books. When he's not painting or drawing, he likes hiking, biking, and drinking milk from the carton. He lives in the mountains of Utah with his wife and kids, and their black dog named Blue.

How much do you know about

Eerie Elementary

The End of ORSON EERIE?

In Chapter One, pumpkins attack in the lunchroom! How is this battle against Orson Eerie different from previous battles? Find **two** differences.

Jasper Eerie tells Sam he had a nightmare about an army of Orson Eeries. Jasper's nightmare gives Sam an idea for an army of his own. What is Sam's plan?

What gift does Mr. Nekobi give the hall monitors?

The hall monitor sash is a symbol of friendship and goodness. Why does the power of the sash hurt Orson Eerie? Reread pages 81–82.

The hall monitors have battled different forms of Orson Eerie. Which version of Orson Eerie would **you** want to battle? How would you defeat him? Use text and art to create your battle scene.